T0380847

The Adventures of Holly Hill Sticks in the Snow

Written by Gloria Sherman

Illustrated by Susan Shorter

AuthorHouse™
1663 Liberty Drive
Bloomington, IN 47403
www.authorhouse.com
Phone: 1-800-839-8640

Published by AuthorHouse 02/27/2013

ISBN: 978-1-4817-1027-5 (sc)
           978-1-4817-1028-2 (e)

Library of Congress Control Number: 2013901233

Any people depicted in stock imagery provided by Thinkstock are models,
and such images are being used for illustrative purposes only.
Certain stock imagery © Thinkstock.

This book is printed on acid-free paper.

authorHOUSE®

Dedicated to Ellie and Katie who loved to run and play in the woods on Holly Hill.

Special love to Steve, Daniel, and Kevin for the happiness you have brought into my life. Best wishes to all of the students I have been lucky enough to teach and work with during my career.

KEEP READING!

TIPS TO BARK ABOUT BEFORE YOU READ... Take time to think about or discuss these important STORY ELEMENTS ...

AUTHOR: Who is the author? What do you know about the author?

ILLUSTRATOR: Who is the illustrator?

SETTING: Look at the front cover of the book. Read the information on the back cover. Where does the story take place? What does Holly Hill look like? Where is it located?

VOCABULARY: -boast, rustle, soothe, pounce, examine, investigate, encourage, prance, coax

"Come on Katie!" barks Holly. "It's a snow day! Let's wake Daisy and head for the woods."

Holly Hill is covered in a thick blanket of white fluffy powder. The dark green leaves and red berries on the holly trees boast of color with their waxy shine. The hardwood trees crack and squeak as the cool wind gently rustles through the woods.

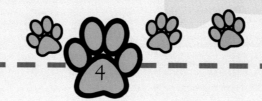

Holly is ready to go outside and play. Katie is perfectly happy to remain on the warm soothing rug. "I'll just stay inside and enjoy the warmth of the fire," replies Katie with a lazy groan. "You and Daisy feel free to explore without me."

Daisy is eager to see what all of the fuss and excitement is about. She wastes no time pouncing off of her favorite chair to join Holly. The house is filled with loud barks as they announce that it is time to go outside.

The door opens just enough to let them outside and keep the warmth in. Daisy rushes to get out before Holly. She cannot wait a minute longer! The cool wind feels so refreshing on her face. The woods are peaceful and calm.

Holly inspects the snow by sniffing and examining it as she walks around. Daisy is very curious, but she is also cautious. She takes a little more time to investigate the change that has taken place. After sticking her nose down deep into the snow, it turns from black to white. With a few shakes, Daisy's black nose returns. She watches Holly and is happy to have her friend to explore with her.

Sticks have always been easy to find on Holly Hill. Daisy is puzzled. She doesn't see any sticks. "Where are the sticks?" barks Daisy. Holly quickly responds with loud barks of encouragement, "Don't give up Daisy, keep looking!" Daisy continues to search by digging deep into the snow until she finds one!

The game begins! "This is my stick," barks Daisy.

"I will get it and chew it up," responds Holly as she watches Daisy prance proudly around the yard. She lets Daisy enjoy her special prize for just a minute and then…

Holly runs after Daisy and quickly grabs one end of the stick with her teeth. She pulls and pulls on the stick and tries to remove it from Daisy's mouth. Daisy tugs harder and harder! After chasing each other around the yard and finding more sticks hidden in the snow, they are too tired to play any longer.

Following a few coaxing barks and whines, the door opens to welcome them back inside. They cuddle up together to the sound of the crackling fire for a very long nap. Their coats are warmed by the fire while they sleep peacefully, and dream of more exciting adventures awaiting them on Holly Hill.

MORE TIPS TO BARK ABOUT...

CHARACTERS: Describe the main characters in the story. Who was your favorite character? Why?

THEME: What was the theme of the story?

Think of a friend you enjoy spending time with. What makes that person special?

Thanks for sharing in the fun on Holly Hill!

Contact Information

hollyhill2013@yahoo.com

PARENT/SCHOOL/COMMUNITY LITERACY EVENTS-
pals4literacy@yahoo.com

 Visit us on FaceBook at www.facebook.com/The Adventures of Holly Hill